bonus!

LOOKING FOR MORE OPPORTUNITIES FOR YOUR PRESCHOOLER?

DOWNLOAD OUR FREE PRESCHOOL TEACHER'S GUIDE AT:

GENTLECLASSICALPRESCHOOL.COM

USING THE PRESCHOOL DAILY CHECK-UP

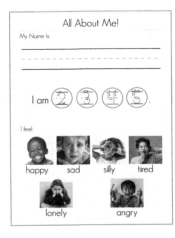

All About Me is designed to help our children practice writing their name, identifying their age, and evaluating their emotional state. The lined space for the name works best with children under 4 if you write their name with a highlighter and then allow them to trace it. For children 4 and over, you can begin allowing them to write their name with more independence, once you believe they are ready to do so.

I know what today is! is designed to facilitate consistent practice of the days of the weeks and months of the year. For children 3 and under, expect that this is a long-term goal and enjoy the process. The first letter of the week is emboldened for children who can begin to identify each weekday by it's initial letter sound.

We enjoy the days and months songs found free at: *goodandbeautiful.com/ mathhelps*

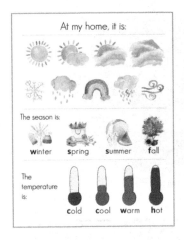

At my home, it is: is designed help our children develop an awareness of the world around them. This results in basic life skills like dressing properly for the weather. Seasonal rhythms are important to mark, especially in preschool. This simple page prompts a quick visit out the door to take a look at the sky and experience ambient temperatures outside. We also track the current season. Consider celebrating seasonal changes with small celebrations.

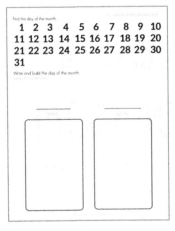

Optional: Find/Write/Build the day of the month is designed for children who are at least 3 years of age. On this page, we identify the day of the month using a traditional home calendar and have them find it on the page. The next step is that they write that day onto the blank spaces. At 3-years-old, you might note that in the number 19, the one is in the tens place and the 9 is in the ones place and help them write them in the proper space. However, while this will holds essentially no meaning to them, you will be creating foundational skills that they will develop understanding for later. In our 19, example, using unit and tens sticks, help them place one "ten" into the tens box and nine "ones" into the ones box. Most children will need to be around 4 before they grasp this concept.

EXAMPLES

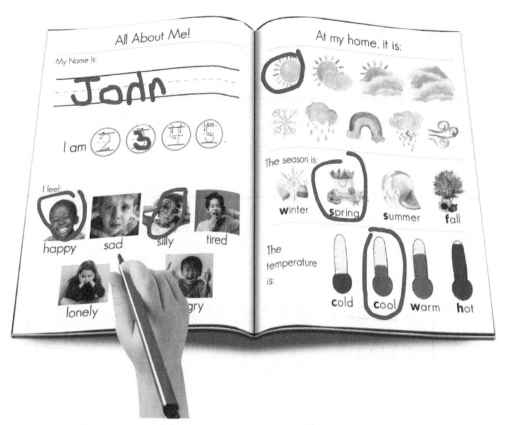

You can find base ten blocks on Amazon or other educational retailers.

All About Me!

My Name Is:

_____

— — — — — — — — — — — — — — —

_____

I am  .

I feel:

happy   sad   silly   tired

lonely   angry

At my home, it is:

The season is:

winter

spring

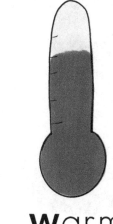

summer

fall

The temperature is:

cold   **c**ool   **w**arm   **h**ot

I know what today is!

O**S**unday   O**M**onday   O**T**uesday

O**W**ednesday   O**Th**ursday

O**F**riday   O**S**aturday

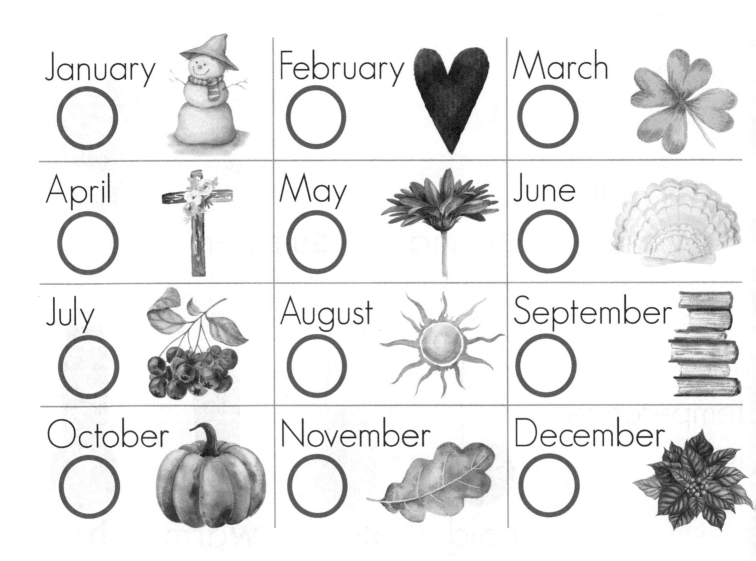

January O	February O	March O
April O	May O	June O
July O	August O	September O
October O	November O	December O

Find the day of the month:

1   2   3   4   5   6   7   8   9   10
11 12 13 14 15 16 17 18 19 20
21 22 23 24 25 26 27 28 29 30
31

Write and build the day of the month:
(using unit and ten blocks)

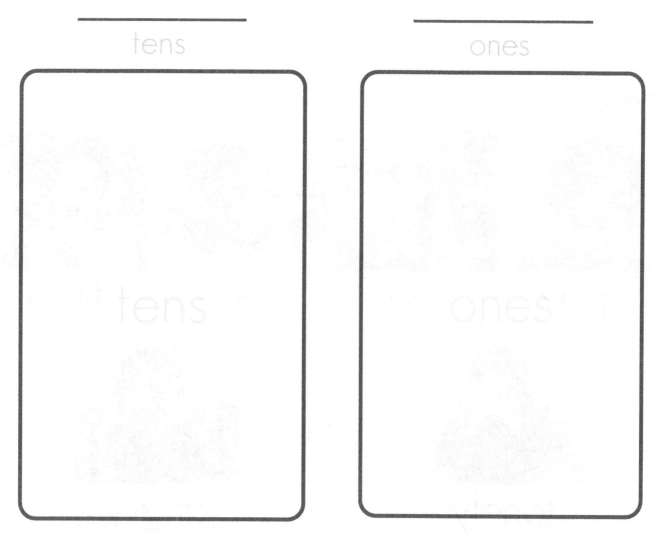

_____   _____
tens   ones

tens   ones

All About Me!

My Name Is:

_____

- - - - - - - - - - - - - - - - -

_____

I am 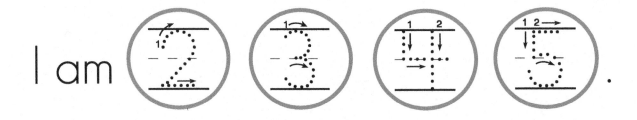.

I feel:

happy　　　sad　　　silly　　　tired

lonely　　　　　　angry

At my home, it is:

The season is:

winter   **s**pring   **s**ummer   **f**all

The temperature is:

cold   **c**ool   **w**arm   **h**ot

I know what today is!

○ **S**unday ○ **M**onday ○ **T**uesday

○ **W**ednesday ○ **Th**ursday

○ **F**riday ○ **S**aturday

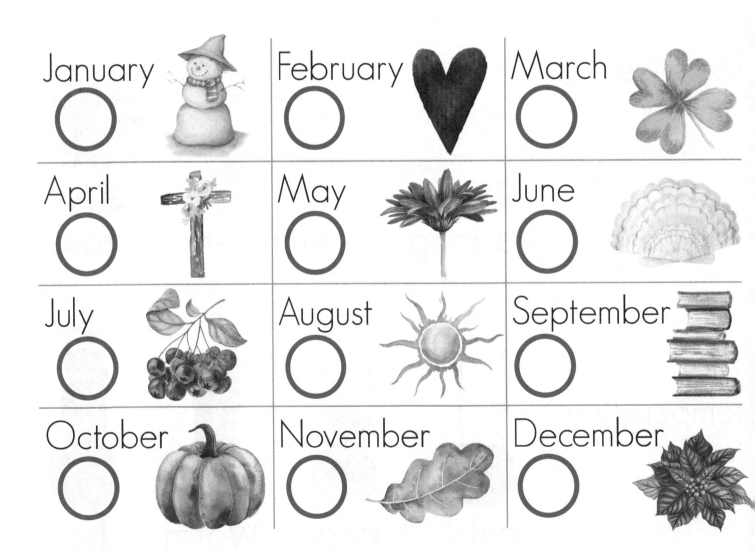

January ○	February ○	March ○
April ○	May ○	June ○
July ○	August ○	September ○
October ○	November ○	December ○

Find the day of the month:

1   2   3   4   5   6   7   8   9   10

11   12   13   14   15   16   17   18   19   20

21   22   23   24   25   26   27   28   29   30

31

Write and build the day of the month:
(using unit and ten blocks)

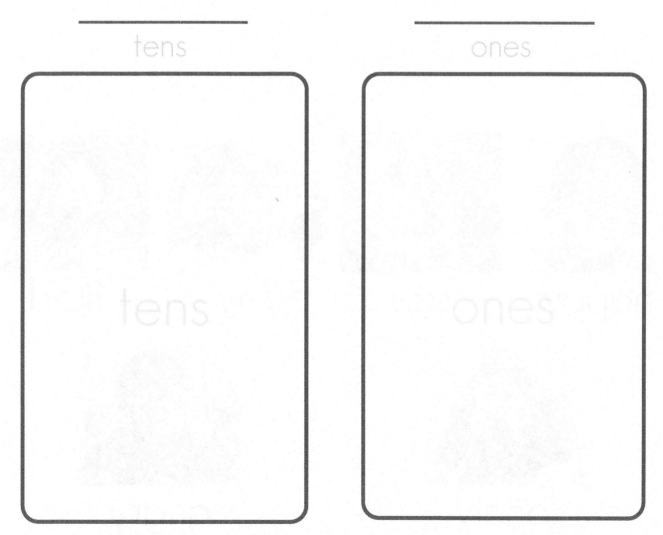

tens   ones

tens   ones

All About Me!

My Name Is:

_____

- - - - - - - - - - - - - - - - -

_____

I am 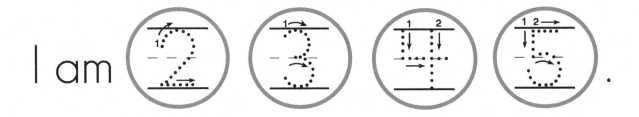 .

I feel:

happy   sad   silly   tired

lonely   angry

At my home, it is:

The season is:

winter **s**pring **s**ummer **f**all

The temperature is:

cold **c**ool **w**arm **h**ot

I know what today is!

○ **S**unday ○ **M**onday ○ **T**uesday

○ **W**ednesday ○ **Th**ursday

○ **F**riday ○ **S**aturday

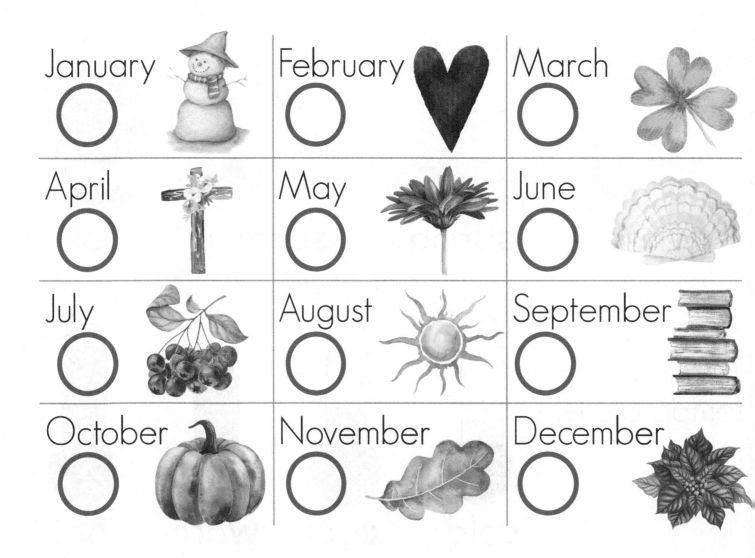

January ○	February ○	March ○
April ○	May ○	June ○
July ○	August ○	September ○
October ○	November ○	December ○

Find the day of the month:

**1 2 3 4 5 6 7 8 9 10
11 12 13 14 15 16 17 18 19 20
21 22 23 24 25 26 27 28 29 30
31**

Write and build the day of the month:
(using unit and ten blocks)

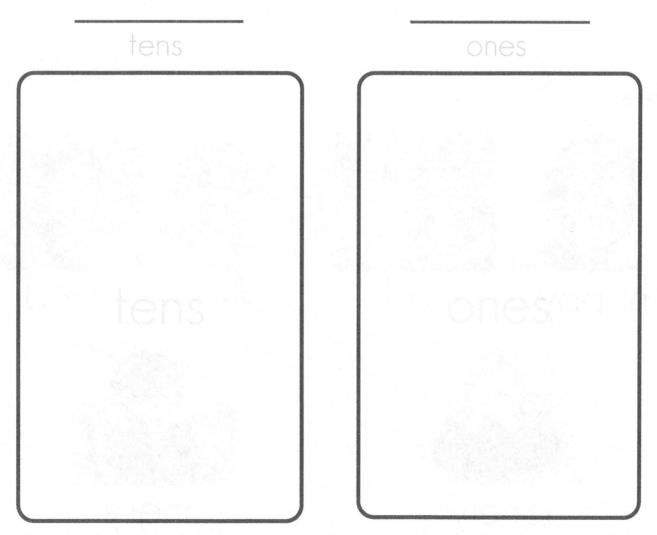

_____
tens

_____
ones

All About Me!

My Name Is:

_____

- - - - - - - - - - - - - - - - -

_____

I am 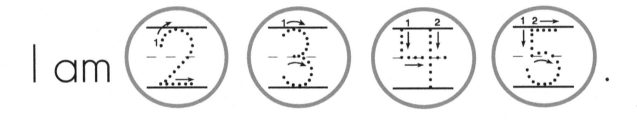 .

I feel:

happy

sad

silly

tired

lonely

angry

At my home, it is:

The season is:

winter

spring

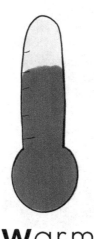

summer

fall

The temperature is:

cold

cool

warm

hot

I know what today is!

◯**S**unday ◯**M**onday ◯**T**uesday

◯**W**ednesday ◯**Th**ursday

◯**F**riday ◯**S**aturday

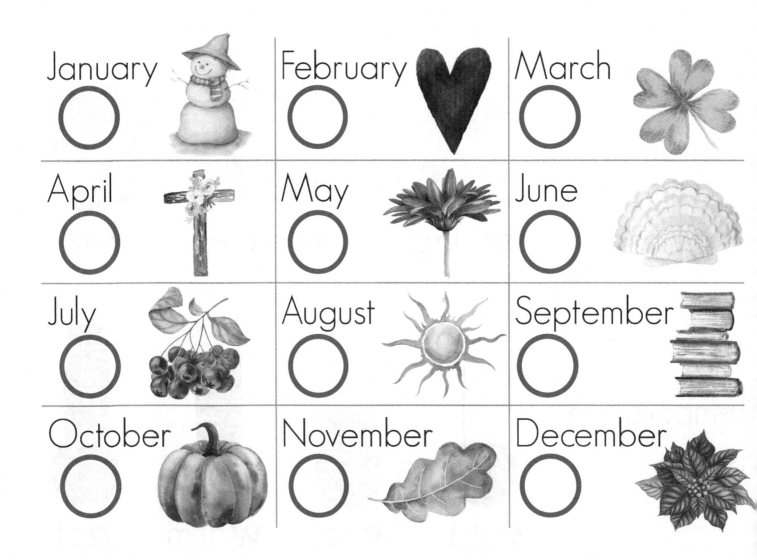

January ◯	February ◯	March ◯
April ◯	May ◯	June ◯
July ◯	August ◯	September ◯
October ◯	November ◯	December ◯

Find the day of the month:

1 2 3 4 5 6 7 8 9 10
11 12 13 14 15 16 17 18 19 20
21 22 23 24 25 26 27 28 29 30
31

Write and build the day of the month:
(using unit and ten blocks)

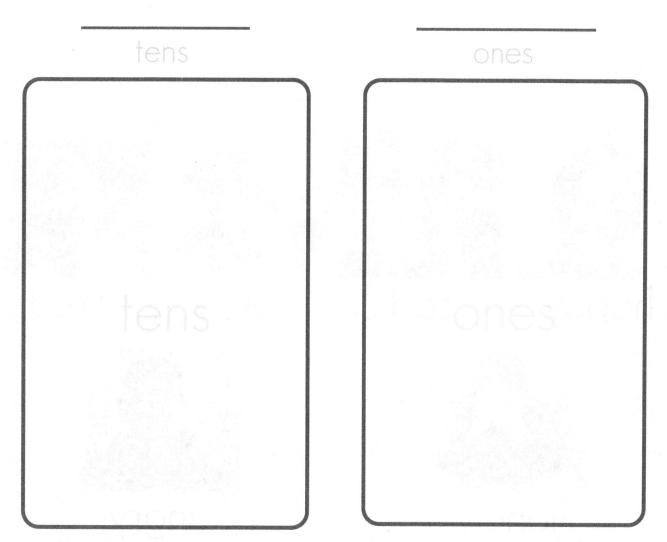

_____   _____
tens   ones

All About Me!

My Name Is:

_____

- - - - - - - - - - - - - - - -

_____

I am .

I feel:

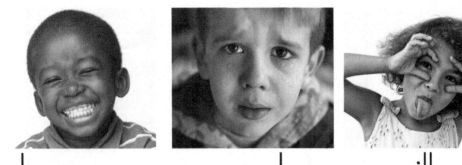

happy   sad   silly   tired

lonely

angry

At my home, it is:

The season is:

 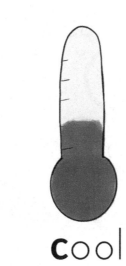 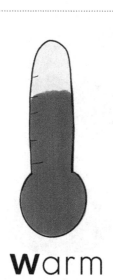 

winter   **s**pring   **s**ummer   **f**all

The temperature is:

cold   **c**ool   **w**arm   **h**ot

I know what today is!

◯**S**unday ◯**M**onday ◯**T**uesday

◯**W**ednesday ◯**Th**ursday

◯**F**riday ◯**S**aturday

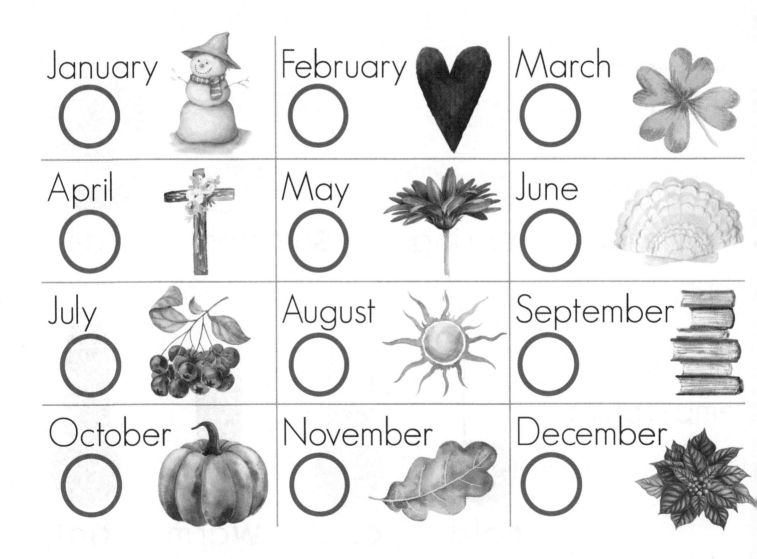

January ◯	February ◯	March ◯
April ◯	May ◯	June ◯
July ◯	August ◯	September ◯
October ◯	November ◯	December ◯

Find the day of the month:

1   2   3   4   5   6   7   8   9   10

11 12 13 14 15 16 17 18 19 20

21 22 23 24 25 26 27 28 29 30

31

Write and build the day of the month:
(using unit and ten blocks)

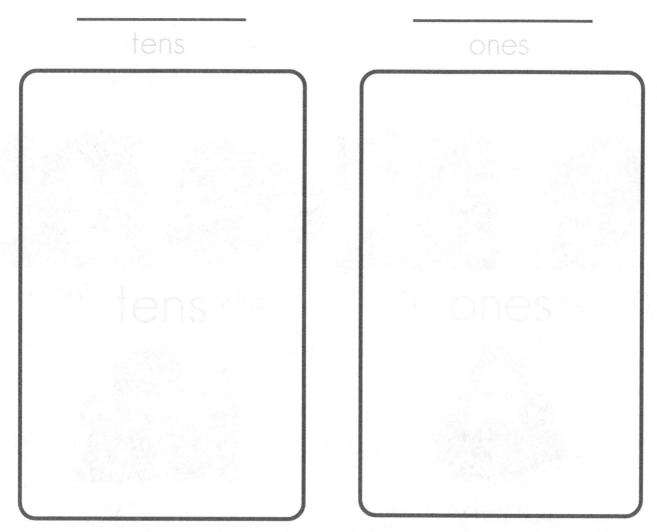

_____   _____

tens   ones

All About Me!

My Name Is:

_____

– – – – – – – – – – – – – – – – – –

_____

I am  .

I feel:

happy   sad   silly   tired

lonely   angry

At my home, it is:

The season is:

  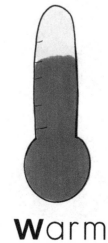 

winter   **s**pring   **s**ummer   **f**all

The temperature is:

  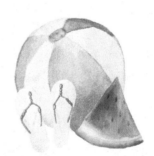 

cold   **c**ool   **w**arm   **h**ot

I know what today is!

○ **S**unday ○ **M**onday ○ **T**uesday

○ **W**ednesday ○ **Th**ursday

○ **F**riday ○ **S**aturday

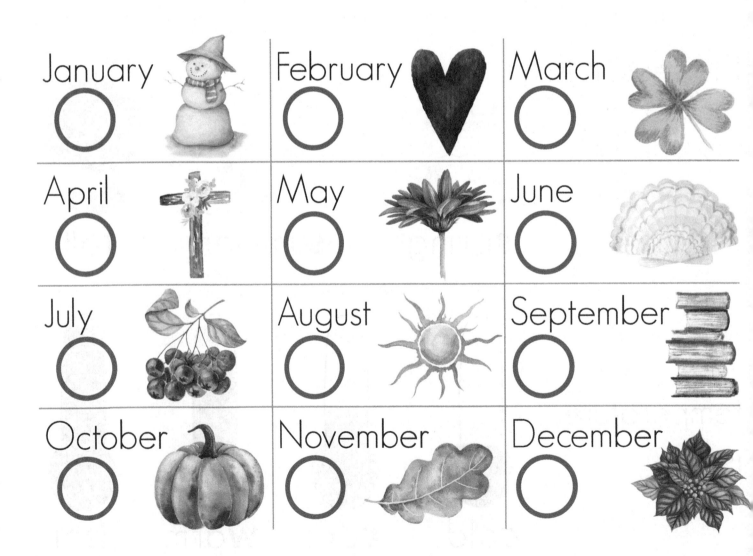

January ○	February ○	March ○
April ○	May ○	June ○
July ○	August ○	September ○
October ○	November ○	December ○

Find the day of the month:

1 2 3 4 5 6 7 8 9 10
11 12 13 14 15 16 17 18 19 20
21 22 23 24 25 26 27 28 29 30
31

Write and build the day of the month:
(using unit and ten blocks)

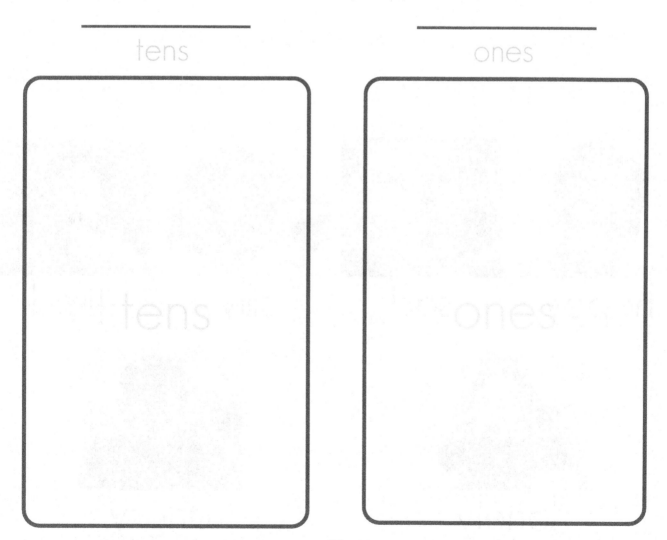

tens

ones

All About Me!

My Name Is:

_____

I am 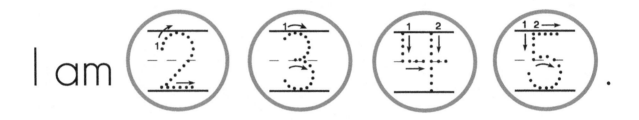.

I feel:

happy   sad   silly   tired

lonely   angry

At my home, it is:

The season is:

winter

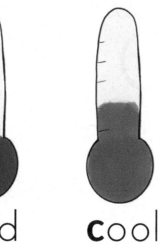

spring

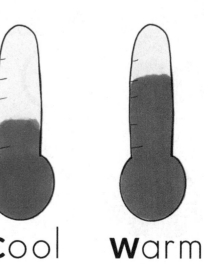

summer

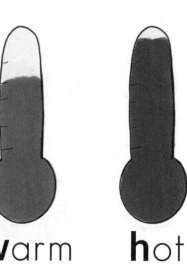

fall

The temperature is:

cold   **c**ool   **w**arm   **h**ot

I know what today is!

◯**S**unday ◯**M**onday ◯**T**uesday

◯**W**ednesday ◯**Th**ursday

◯**F**riday ◯**S**aturday

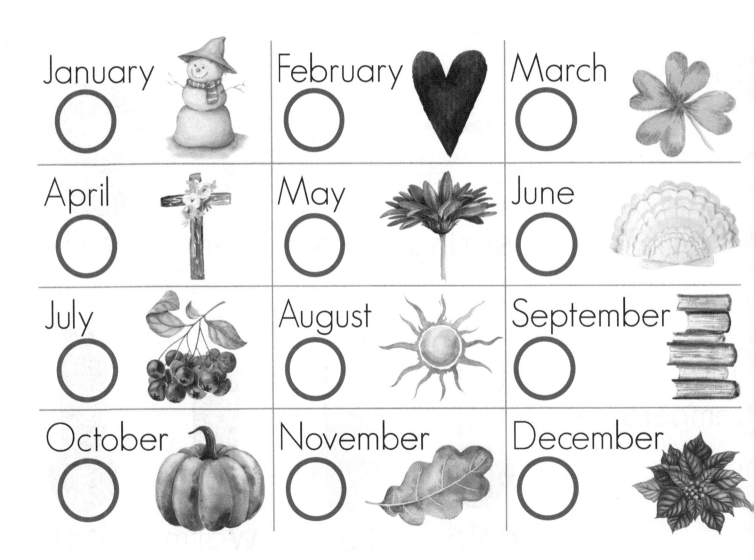

January ◯	February ◯	March ◯
April ◯	May ◯	June ◯
July ◯	August ◯	September ◯
October ◯	November ◯	December ◯

Find the day of the month:

1 2 3 4 5 6 7 8 9 10
11 12 13 14 15 16 17 18 19 20
21 22 23 24 25 26 27 28 29 30
31

Write and build the day of the month:
(using unit and ten blocks)

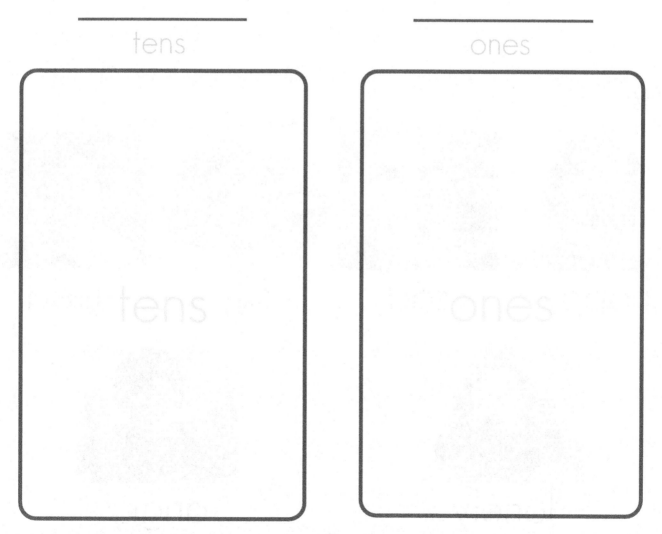

_____   _____
tens   ones

All About Me!

My Name Is:

_____

I am  .

I feel:

happy   sad   silly   tired

lonely

angry

At my home, it is:

The season is:

winter   **s**pring   **s**ummer   **f**all

The temperature is:

cold   **c**ool   **w**arm   **h**ot

I know what today is!

◯**S**unday　◯**M**onday　◯**T**uesday

◯**W**ednesday　◯**Th**ursday

◯**F**riday　◯**S**aturday

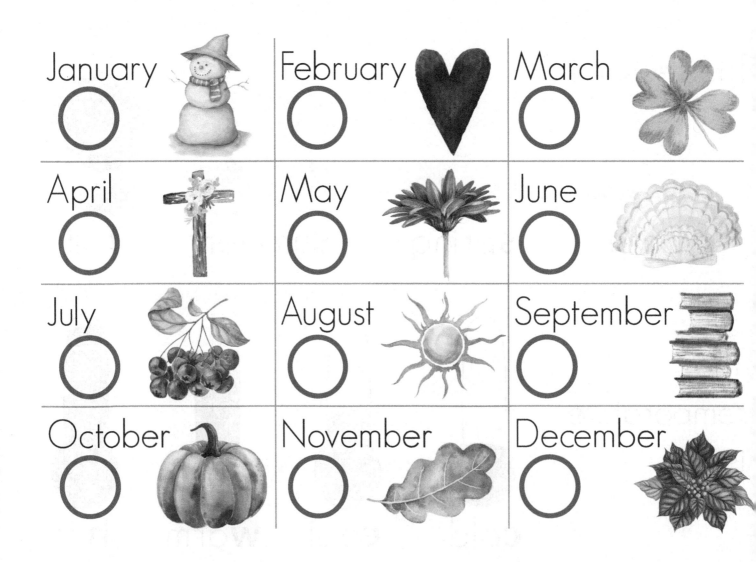

January	February	March
◯	◯	◯
April	May	June
◯	◯	◯
July	August	September
◯	◯	◯
October	November	December
◯	◯	◯

Find the day of the month:

1   2   3   4   5   6   7   8   9   10
11 12 13 14 15 16 17 18 19 20
21 22 23 24 25 26 27 28 29 30
31

Write and build the day of the month:
(using unit and ten blocks)

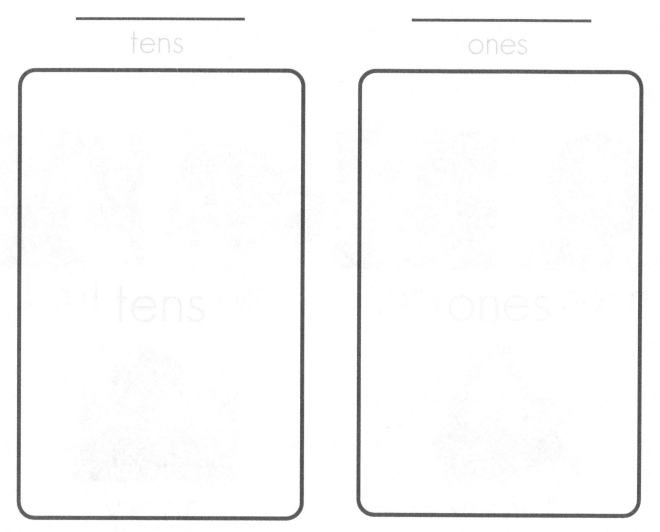

_____   _____
tens   ones

All About Me!

My Name Is:

_____

– – – – – – – – – – – – – – – – –

_____

I am 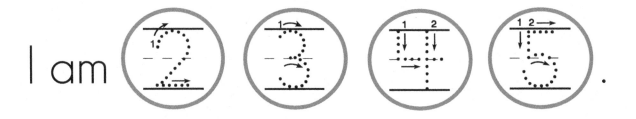 .

I feel:

happy   sad   silly   tired

lonely   angry

At my home, it is:

The season is:

  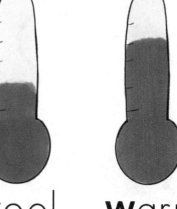 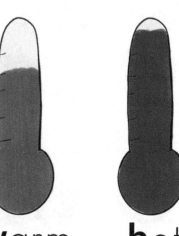

winter   **s**pring   **s**ummer   **f**all

The temperature is:

cold   **c**ool   **w**arm   **h**ot

I know what today is!

○**S**unday ○**M**onday ○**T**uesday

○**W**ednesday ○**Th**ursday

○**F**riday ○**S**aturday

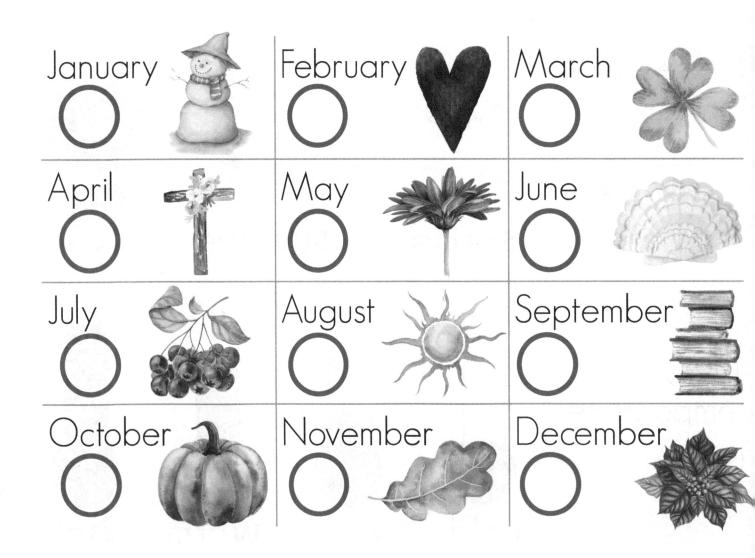

January ○	February ○	March ○
April ○	May ○	June ○
July ○	August ○	September ○
October ○	November ○	December ○

Find the day of the month:

1 2 3 4 5 6 7 8 9 10
11 12 13 14 15 16 17 18 19 20
21 22 23 24 25 26 27 28 29 30
31

Write and build the day of the month:
(using unit and ten blocks)

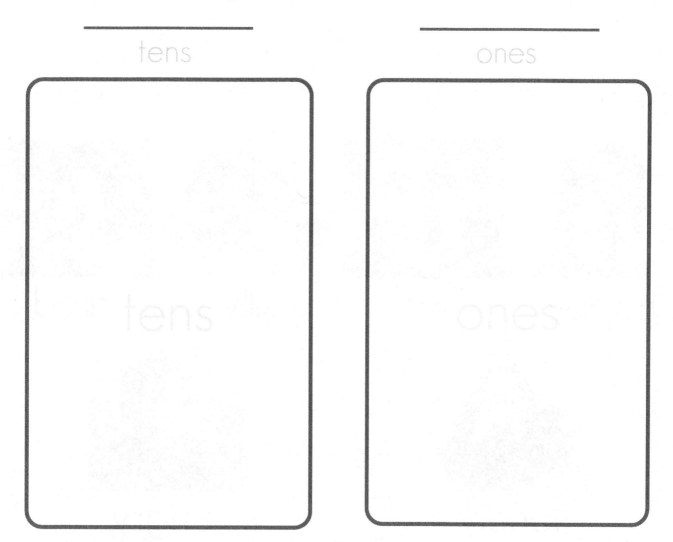

_____   _____
tens   ones

All About Me!

My Name Is:

_____

- - - - - - - - - - - - - - - - -

_____

I am  .

I feel:

happy   sad   silly   tired

lonely   angry

At my home, it is:

The season is:

winter

spring

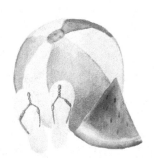

summer

fall

The temperature is:

cold

cool

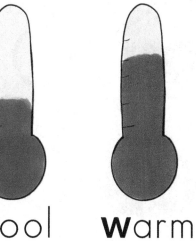

warm

hot

I know what today is!

◯**S**unday ◯**M**onday ◯**T**uesday

◯**W**ednesday ◯**Th**ursday

◯**F**riday ◯**S**aturday

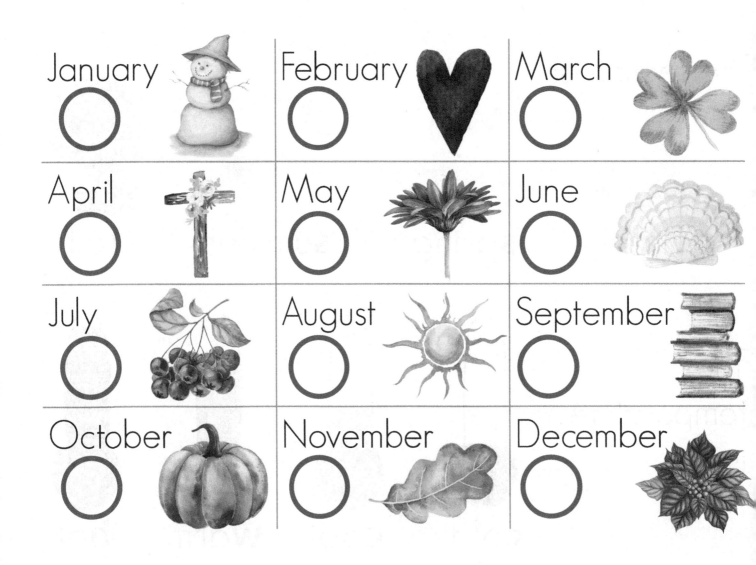

January ◯	February ◯	March ◯
April ◯	May ◯	June ◯
July ◯	August ◯	September ◯
October ◯	November ◯	December ◯

Find the day of the month:

1   2   3   4   5   6   7   8   9   10

11 12 13 14 15 16 17 18 19 20

21 22 23 24 25 26 27 28 29 30

31

Write and build the day of the month:
(using unit and ten blocks)

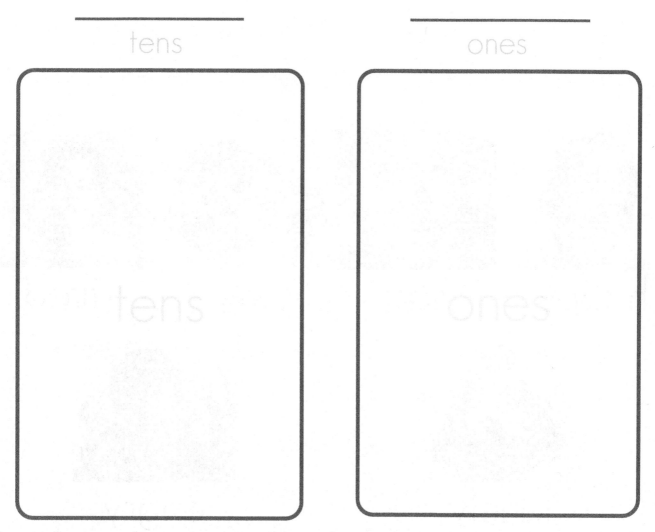

_____   _____
tens   ones

tens   ones

All About Me!

My Name Is:

_____

— — — — — — — — — — — — — — — — —

_____

I am  .

I feel:

| happy | sad | silly | tired |

lonely

angry

At my home, it is:

The season is:

winter

spring

summer

fall

The temperature is:

cold   **c**ool   **w**arm   **h**ot

I know what today is!

◯**S**unday ◯**M**onday ◯**T**uesday

◯**W**ednesday ◯**Th**ursday

◯**F**riday ◯**S**aturday

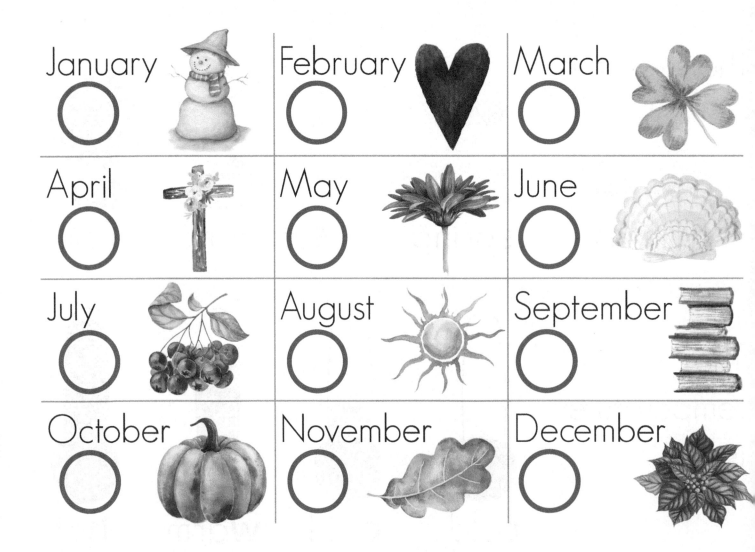

January ◯	February ◯	March ◯
April ◯	May ◯	June ◯
July ◯	August ◯	September ◯
October ◯	November ◯	December ◯

Find the day of the month:

1 2 3 4 5 6 7 8 9 10
11 12 13 14 15 16 17 18 19 20
21 22 23 24 25 26 27 28 29 30
31

Write and build the day of the month:
(using unit and ten blocks)

_____   _____
tens   ones

All About Me!

My Name Is:

_____

- - - - - - - - - - - - - - - - -

_____

I am  .

I feel:

happy   sad   silly   tired

lonely

angry

At my home, it is:

The season is:

winter

spring

summer

fall

The temperature is:

cold   cool   warm   hot

I know what today is!

◯**S**unday   ◯**M**onday   ◯**T**uesday

◯**W**ednesday   ◯**Th**ursday

◯**F**riday   ◯**S**aturday

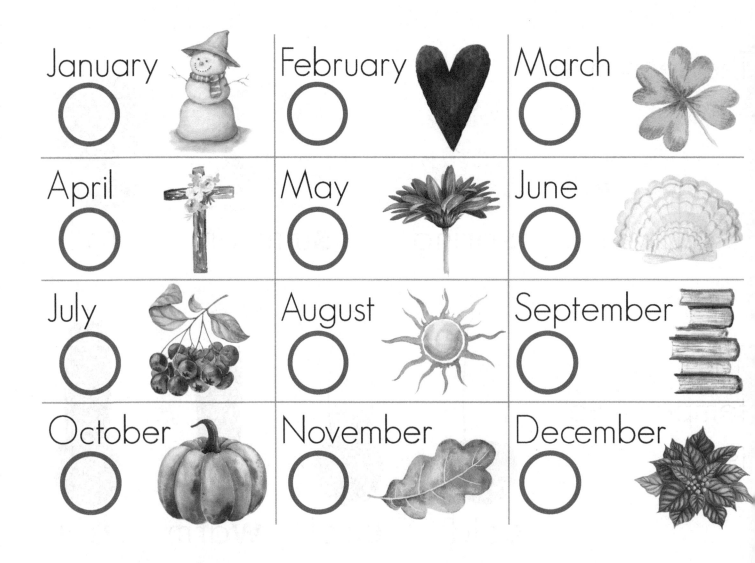

January ◯	February ◯	March ◯
April ◯	May ◯	June ◯
July ◯	August ◯	September ◯
October ◯	November ◯	December ◯

Find the day of the month:

1 2 3 4 5 6 7 8 9 10
11 12 13 14 15 16 17 18 19 20
21 22 23 24 25 26 27 28 29 30
31

Write and build the day of the month:
(using unit and ten blocks)

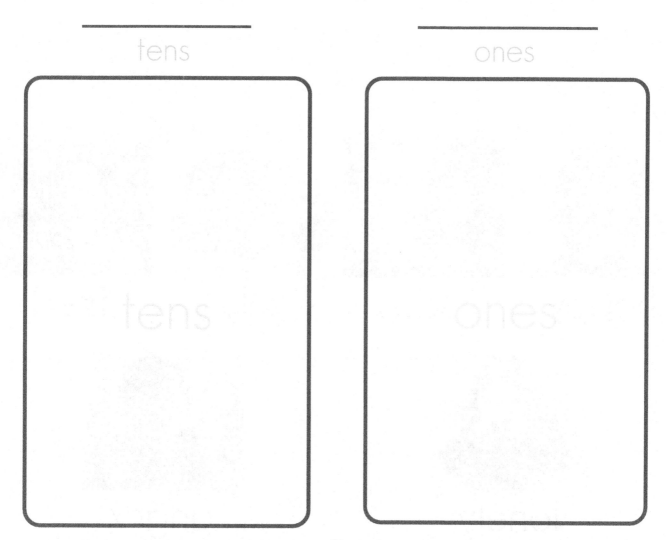

_____   _____
tens   ones

All About Me!

My Name Is:

_____

- - - - - - - - - - - - - - - - - -

_____

I am .

I feel:

happy   sad   silly   tired

lonely   angry

At my home, it is:

The season is:

winter   **s**pring   **s**ummer   **f**all

The temperature is:

cold   **c**ool   **w**arm   **h**ot

I know what today is!

○ **S**unday   ○ **M**onday   ○ **T**uesday

○ **W**ednesday   ○ **Th**ursday

○ **F**riday   ○ **S**aturday

January ○	February ○	March ○
April ○	May ○	June ○
July ○	August ○	September ○
October ○	November ○	December ○

Find the day of the month:

1   2   3   4   5   6   7   8   9   10
11 12 13 14 15 16 17 18 19 20
21 22 23 24 25 26 27 28 29 30
31

Write and build the day of the month:
(using unit and ten blocks)

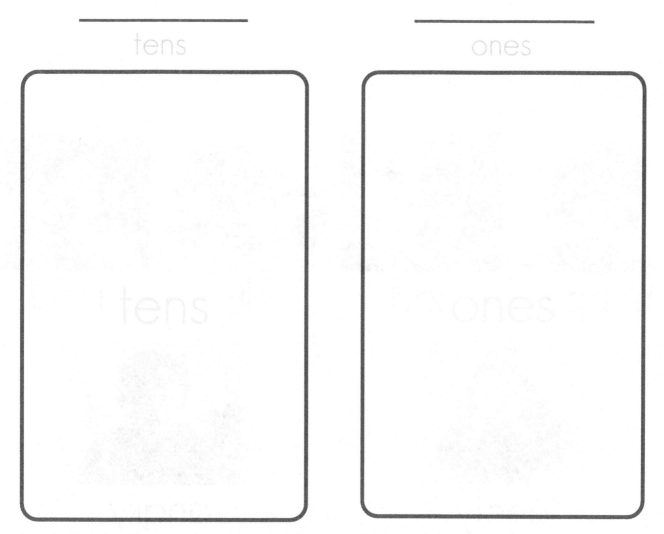

_____   _____
tens   ones

55

All About Me!

My Name Is:

_____

- - - - - - - - - - - - - - - -

_____

I am  .

I feel:

happy   sad   silly   tired

lonely   angry

At my home, it is:

The season is:

winter

spring

summer

fall

The temperature is:

cold   **c**ool   **w**arm   **h**ot

I know what today is!

○ **S**unday ○ **M**onday ○ **T**uesday

○ **W**ednesday ○ **Th**ursday

○ **F**riday ○ **S**aturday

January ○	February ○	March ○
April ○	May ○	June ○
July ○	August ○	September ○
October ○	November ○	December ○

Find the day of the month:

1 2 3 4 5 6 7 8 9 10
11 12 13 14 15 16 17 18 19 20
21 22 23 24 25 26 27 28 29 30
31

Write and build the day of the month:
(using unit and ten blocks)

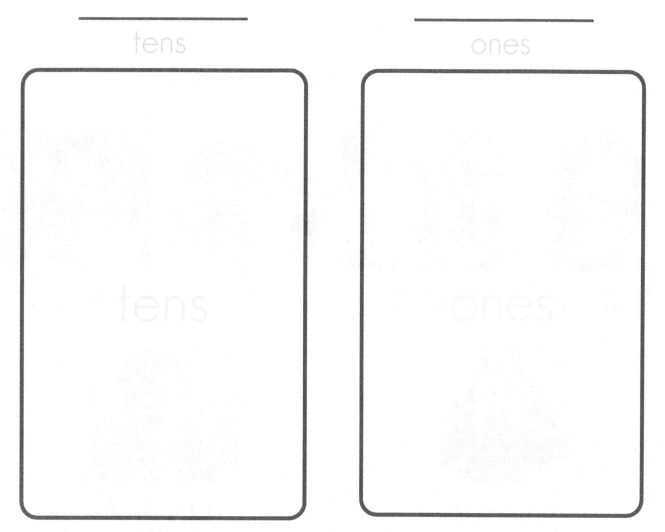

tens   ones

All About Me!

My Name Is:

_____

- - - - - - - - - - - - - - - - -

_____

I am  .

I feel:

happy   sad   silly   tired

lonely   angry

At my home, it is:

The season is:

winter   **s**pring   **s**ummer   **f**all

The temperature is:

cold   **c**ool   **w**arm   **h**ot

I know what today is!

○**S**unday ○**M**onday ○**T**uesday

○**W**ednesday ○**Th**ursday

○**F**riday ○**S**aturday

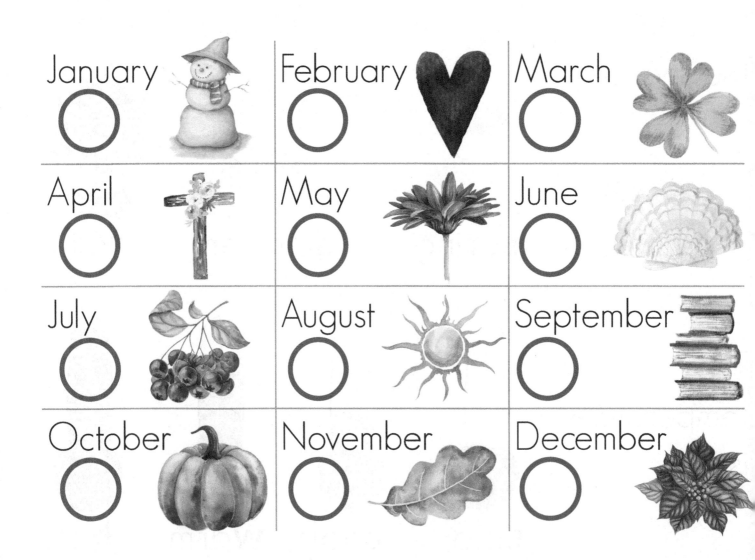

January ○	February ○	March ○
April ○	May ○	June ○
July ○	August ○	September ○
October ○	November ○	December ○

Find the day of the month:

1   2   3   4   5   6   7   8   9   10
11 12 13 14 15 16 17 18 19 20
21 22 23 24 25 26 27 28 29 30
31

Write and build the day of the month:
(using unit and ten blocks)

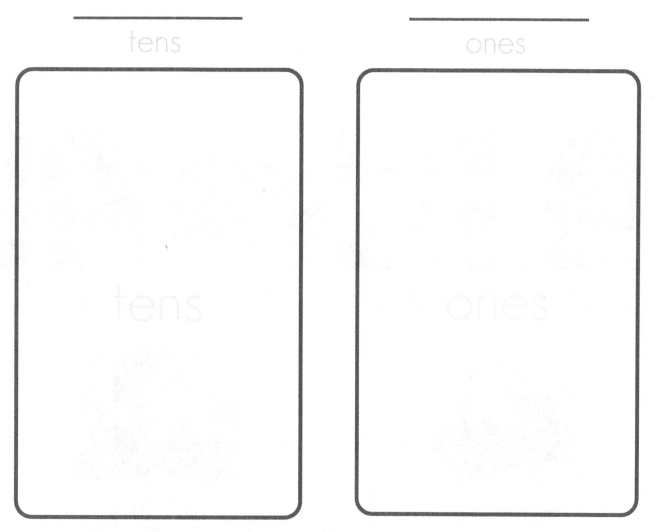

_____   _____
tens   ones

tens   ones

All About Me!

My Name Is:

_____

- - - - - - - - - - - - - - - - - -

_____

I am  .

I feel:

happy   sad   silly   tired

lonely   angry

At my home, it is:

The season is:

winter **s**pring **s**ummer **f**all

The temperature is:

cold **c**ool **w**arm **h**ot

I know what today is!

○ **S**unday ○ **M**onday ○ **T**uesday

○ **W**ednesday ○ **Th**ursday

○ **F**riday ○ **S**aturday

January ○	February ○	March ○
April ○	May ○	June ○
July ○	August ○	September ○
October ○	November ○	December ○

Find the day of the month:

1   2   3   4   5   6   7   8   9   10

11 12 13 14 15 16 17 18 19 20

21 22 23 24 25 26 27 28 29 30

31

Write and build the day of the month:
(using unit and ten blocks)

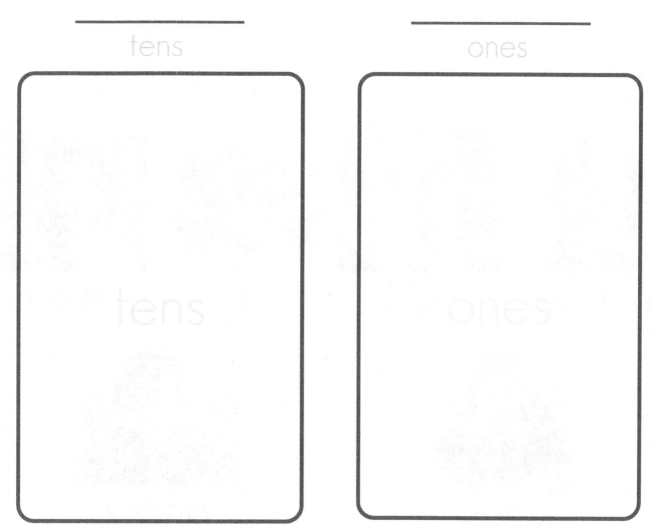

tens   ones

All About Me!

My Name Is:

_____

I am  .

I feel:

At my home, it is:

The season is:

 **w**inter

 **s**pring

 **s**ummer

 **f**all

The temperature is:

 **c**old

 **c**ool

 **w**arm

 **h**ot

I know what today is!

○ **S**unday　○ **M**onday　○ **T**uesday

○ **W**ednesday　○ **Th**ursday

○ **F**riday　○ **S**aturday

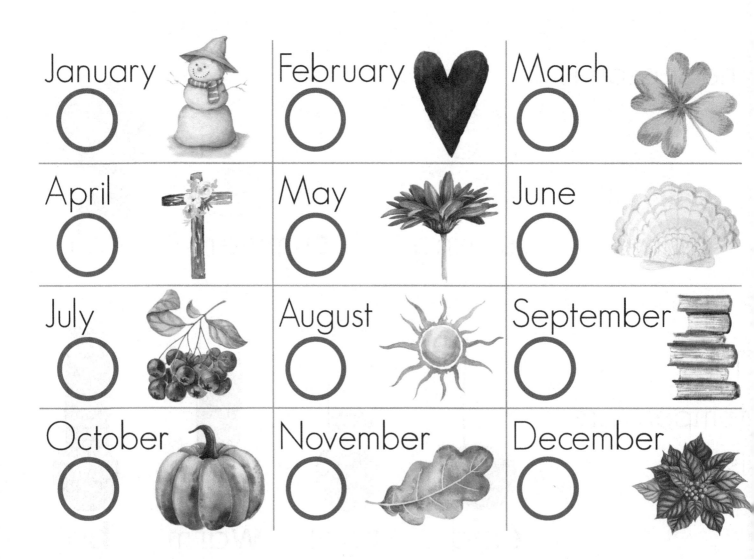

January ○	February ○	March ○
April ○	May ○	June ○
July ○	August ○	September ○
October ○	November ○	December ○

Find the day of the month:

1   2   3   4   5   6   7   8   9   10
11 12 13 14 15 16 17 18 19 20
21 22 23 24 25 26 27 28 29 30
31

Write and build the day of the month:
(using unit and ten blocks)

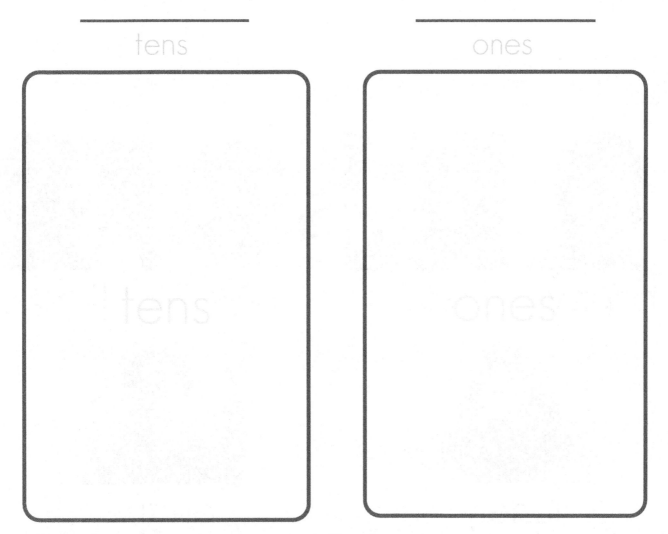

_____   _____
tens   ones

All About Me!

My Name Is:

_____

- - - - - - - - - - - - - - - - - - - -

_____

I am 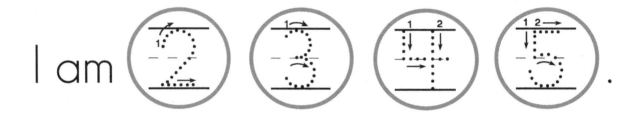 .

I feel:

happy   sad   silly   tired

lonely   angry

At my home, it is:

The season is:

winter   **s**pring   **s**ummer   **f**all

The temperature is:

cold   **c**ool   **w**arm   **h**ot

I know what today is!

◯**S**unday   ◯**M**onday   ◯**T**uesday

◯**W**ednesday   ◯**Th**ursday

◯**F**riday   ◯**S**aturday

January ◯	February ◯	March ◯
April ◯	May ◯	June ◯
July ◯	August ◯	September ◯
October ◯	November ◯	December ◯

Find the day of the month:

1   2   3   4   5   6   7   8   9   10
11 12 13 14 15 16 17 18 19 20
21 22 23 24 25 26 27 28 29 30
31

Write and build the day of the month:
(using unit and ten blocks)

_____   _____
tens   ones

All About Me!

My Name Is:

_____

- - - - - - - - - - - - - - - - -

_____

I am 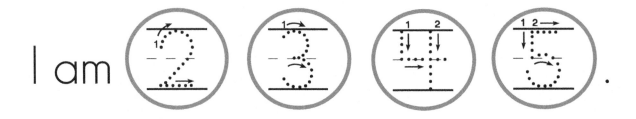 .

I feel:

happy   sad   silly   tired

lonely   angry

At my home, it is:

The season is:

winter

spring

summer

fall

The temperature is:

cold   **c**ool   **w**arm   **h**ot

I know what today is!

◯**S**unday ◯**M**onday ◯**T**uesday

◯**W**ednesday ◯**Th**ursday

◯**F**riday ◯**S**aturday

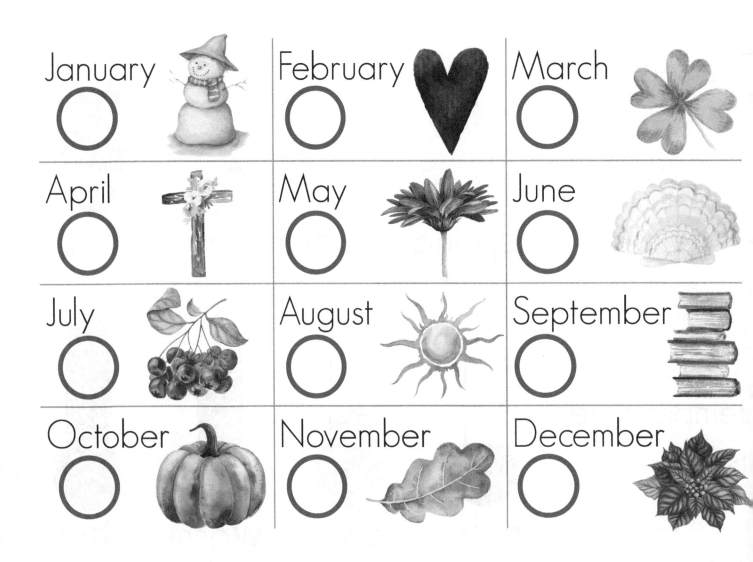

January ◯	February ◯	March ◯
April ◯	May ◯	June ◯
July ◯	August ◯	September ◯
October ◯	November ◯	December ◯

Find the day of the month:

1 2 3 4 5 6 7 8 9 10
11 12 13 14 15 16 17 18 19 20
21 22 23 24 25 26 27 28 29 30
31

Write and build the day of the month:
(using unit and ten blocks)

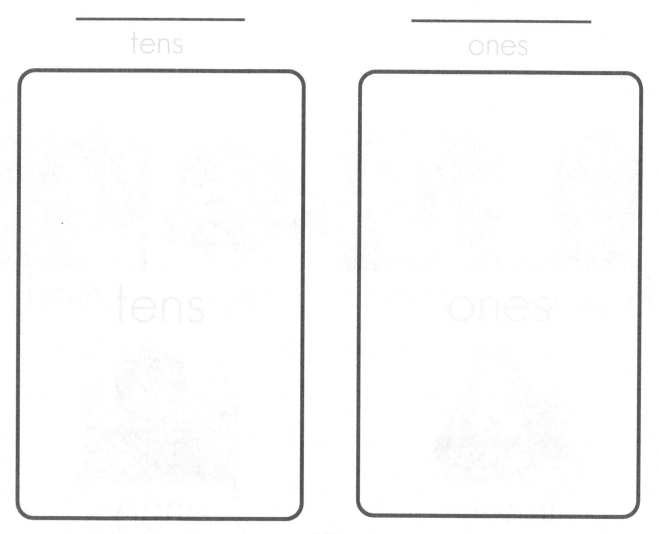

_____   _____
tens   ones

All About Me!

My Name Is:

_____

- - - - - - - - - - - - - - - - - -

_____

I am 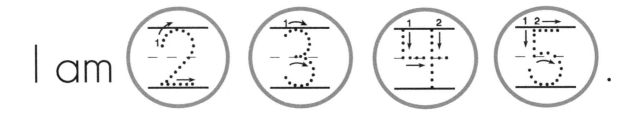 .

I feel:

happy   sad   silly   tired

lonely   angry

At my home, it is:

The season is:

winter

spring

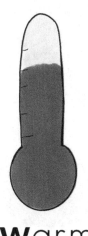

summer

fall

The temperature is:

cold   **c**ool   **w**arm   **h**ot

I know what today is!

○**S**unday ○**M**onday ○**T**uesday

○**W**ednesday ○**Th**ursday

○**F**riday ○**S**aturday

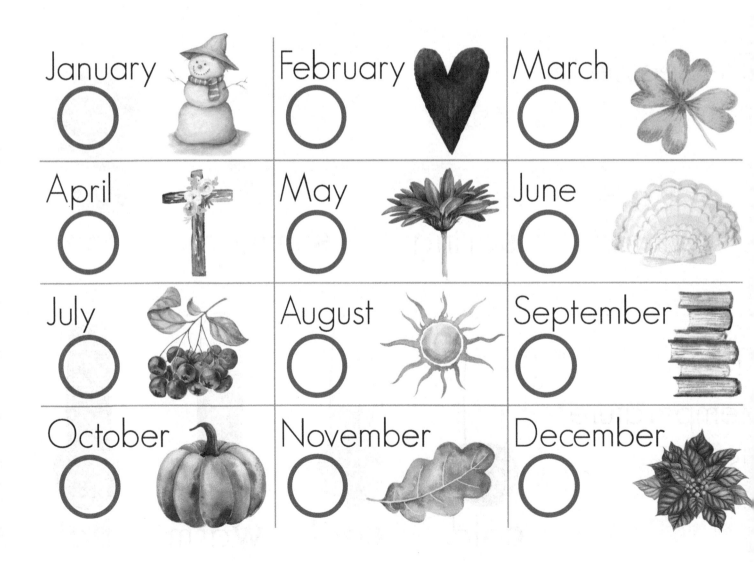

January ○	February ○	March ○
April ○	May ○	June ○
July ○	August ○	September ○
October ○	November ○	December ○

Find the day of the month:

1   2   3   4   5   6   7   8   9 10

11 12 13 14 15 16 17 18 19 20

21 22 23 24 25 26 27 28 29 30

31

Write and build the day of the month:
(using unit and ten blocks)

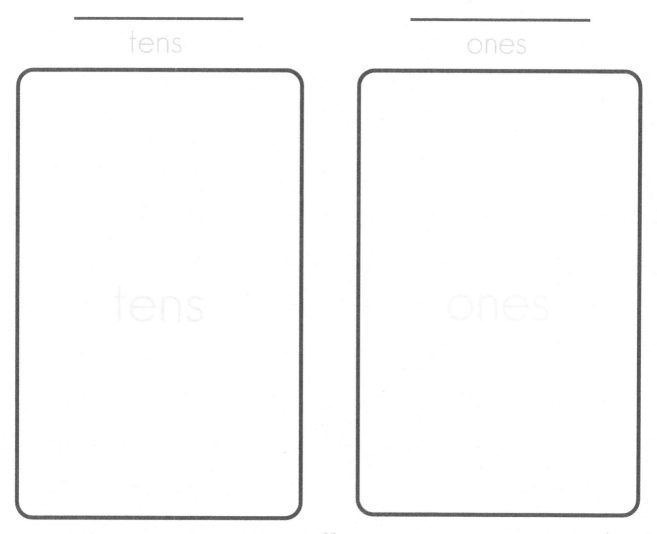

tens   ones

Made in the USA
Coppell, TX
13 December 2024

41994928R00050